A Year at Duck Green

Michaela Morgan
Illustrated by Ian Newsham

MOGGERHANGER
PRIMARY SCHOOL

OXFORD
UNIVERSITY PRESS

January starts the year.
The teachers groan, "Oh dear! Oh dear!"
"My feet are cold!"
"My feet are freezing!"
And Mr Jelly can't stop sneezing!
The teachers like to stay inside,
but Mike and Spike both like to slide.

Ice is nice!

There's ice on the windows,
there's ice on the ground,
there's ice on the trees,
there's ice all around.
There's icicles on bicycles,
icicles in rows,
icicles on drainpipes –
and on Mr Tucker's nose.

February brings the snow.
The teachers groan, "Oh no! Oh no!"
The snow is cold.
The snow is deep.
"Let's make a snowman
and a snow Cheep!"

School is cool!

Look at the snowballs Josh has made,
and there's Mr Tucker – busy with his spade.

In March the days are getting lighter.
The sun is shining, getting brighter.
There is a very windy day,
Leela's kite flies far away.
The leaves blow here,
the leaves blow there.
The leaves are blowing everywhere!

Oh dear me, what a mess they make!
And there's Mr Tucker – busy with his rake.

It's April now. Here come the flowers.
Here comes the sun,
and here come the showers.
The drips start dripping. Drip, drip, drop.
And there's Mr Tucker – busy with his mop.

Poppy gets dry clothes and a cuddle,
when she falls down – **splash** – in a big puddle.

It's May! Hooray! It's school trip day.
What do you think we'll see today?
We'll see the sea,
we'll see some fish.
Everyone has a special wish.
Leela wants to run on the shore.
Buzz wants to see a dinosaur.
Hassan wants to see a shark,
Jo wants to know if dogfish bark.

And the children have another wish.
They **all** want to see a jellyfish!

It's June and it's the School Sports Day.
It's get your shoes and get your shorts day.
Get your egg and get your spoon,
the races all start very soon.
Then Leela jumps and Buzz goes hop.
Jo runs so fast that she can't stop.

Look at Mr Tucker! How fast he goes!
The teachers call him Twinkle Toes.
Twinkle twinkle what a star.
He runs fast and he runs far.

And Josh **won** his race – look at that!
That really is a funny hat!

In July and August there's time to play.
Time to get ready for the holiday.
When the school shuts and everyone's gone,
Mr Tucker carries on.
He's fixing windows, painting walls,
climbing the roof to find lost balls.
He's sweeping, he's cleaning,
he's fixing, he's mopping.
He's busy, busy, busy. He won't be stopping.

He wants the school to be bright and clean.
He wants **everything** to shine inside Duck Green.

September, it's time for school again,
a lot of sun, a bit of rain.
Footprints here and footprints there,
paint on the floor, paint on a chair.

Here a spill, there a spill everywhere a mess.
Did Jo do this? Oh yes, Jo, yes!

October leaves begin to fall,
Mike and Spike like to play football.
Rain fills a drain and falls plip, plip, plop!
Mr Tucker gets busy with his mop!

In November there are fireworks – red, blue
and green –
the brightest lights you've ever seen.
Sparks start to fly and light up the dark,
Mums, dads and children watch in the park.

The nights are getting cold.
In the mornings there is fog.
Kenny's not that keen on fireworks,
but he likes a big hotdog!

It's December and the Christmas play.
Who will be an angel today?
Outside it's cold, the pipes will freeze.
The children sniff, the teachers sneeze.
Everyone is snipping, sticking, painting.
Mr Tucker says, "What **are** they making?"

"Sh!" say the teachers. "Wait and see."
But Mr Tucker wants to know, "What can it be?
What are you making? What a mess!"
Mr Tucker just can't guess.

What are they making? What can it be?
But all they say is, "Wait and see!"

"SURPRISE! SURPRISE! This card's for you.
You've worked so hard the whole year through.
You never, ever make a fuss,
so here's a card with love from us."